Summary:

# Find Your Why

A Practical Guide for Discovering Purpose for
You and Your Team

## By: Simon Sinek, David Mead,
## Peter Docker

**Proudly Brought to you by:**

**Text Copyright © Readtrepreneur**

## Legal & Disclaimer

The information contained in this book is not designed to replace or take the place of any form of medicine or professional medical advice. The information in this book has been provided for educational and entertainment purposes only.

The information contained in this book has been compiled from sources deemed reliable, and it is accurate to the best of the Author's knowledge; however, the Author cannot guarantee its accuracy and validity and cannot be held liable for any errors or omissions. Changes are periodically made to this book. You must consult your doctor or get professional medical advice before using any of the suggested remedies, techniques, or information in this book. Images used in this book is not the same as of that of the actual book. This is a totally separate and different entity from that of the original book titled: "Find Your WHY"

Upon using the information contained in this book, you agree to hold harmless the Author from and against any damages, costs, and expenses, including any legal fees potentially resulting from the application of any of the information provided by this guide. This disclaimer applies to any damages or injury caused by the use and application, whether directly or indirectly, of any advice or information presented, whether for breach of contract, tort, negligence, personal injury, criminal intent, or under any other cause of action.

You agree to accept all risks of using the information presented inside this book. You need to consult a professional medical practitioner to ensure you are both able and healthy enough to participate in this program.

# Table of Contents

# The Book at a Glance

*Find Your WHY* is the much-awaited follow-up book to Simon Sinek's *Start Your WHY*. *Start your WHY* made readers stop and think about their lives, organizations, jobs and businesses and asked the question of WHY they do things in the first place.

In *Find Your WHY*, Sinek collaborated with two other business coaches in order to develop a working handbook on how to apply the principles of finding out WHY people do things, and how to obtain the ultimate fulfillment and satisfaction in everything that they do. If *Start Your WHY* presents the concepts on finding out what your WHY is, *Find Your WHY* almost feels like a workshop to accomplish it.

It is one thing to know WHAT to do, and another thing to know HOW to do it. But the most important aspect in any job, task or project is to know WHY we do it. It is only through knowing our purpose that we can achieve fulfillment in what we do. The authors also make a distinction between fulfillment and happiness and explain WHY fulfillment is much more important.

In *Find Your WHY*, the authors leverage on the successes that Sinek's team had by building upon the concepts presented in

*Start Your WHY*. While he was able to assist organizations and other people on the power of WHY, and was able to successfully argue for its existence, he felt that he still had not helped enough people with his initial book. Together with his team, he was able to find ways to further spread his philosophy. Together, they developed an internet course and the book *Find Your WHY* is the next step in helping people with finding the real purpose and motivation as to why they do things.

With detailed action steps, illustrations, and exercises for each phase of the process, *Find Your WHY* will be great tool to help you tackle many important issues, such as:

* What if my team can't agree on our WHY?

* What if my WHY seems eerily similar to my competitor's?

* If my work doesn't align with my WHY, what steps should I take?

* Can I have more than one WHY?

The authors designed the book as a guide/handbook where they make the concepts available for study and encourage readers to tweak the principles to make them relevant to their specific situations. They encourage team participation in the process to make it more effective. The three appendices are integral to the success of applying the principles of the WHY and readers may find that these sections will be the most referred to parts.

It cannot be emphasized enough that the book must be taken as more of a handbook and guide, rather than a RAH-RAH-RAH motivational tool. While there are certainly more than enough exhortations and inspirational thoughts, the mindset has to be "workbook" all the way.

The primary author of the book, Simon Sinek, is a British-born marketing consultant and motivation speaker, and is the author of four books including the "Why Series". His talk on "How Great Leaders Inspire Action" is rated among the top five most listened-to TED talks of all time, and he is a much sought-after resource person on management and marketing consulting. To add power to the book he enlisted the help of Peter Docker and David Mead as co-authors.

Mr. Docker is a professional pilot and a former senior officer of Britain's Royal Air Force He flew combat flying operations an Air Force Commander and has seen military action all over the world. His Peter was a Force Commander flying combat missions and has seen service across the world. He has taught masteral and doctoral courses at Britain's Defence College; flown the late British Prime Minister Margaret

Thatcher worldwide and has led multi-billion-dollar projects involving procurement and various project negotiations. His specialties include negotiation and crisis management and is also a much sought-after speaker.

Mr. Mead is a long-time associate of Mr. Sinek and has become one of the leading content developers on Mr. Sinek's team. He has been a motivational speaker focusing on corporate culture and leadership since 2012. He has given talks in front of over 150 companies in 5 continents. He holds an MBA with an Organizational Development concentration, and a Bachelors Communications degree.

# FREE BONUSES

### P.S. Is it okay if we overdeliver?

Here at Readtrepreneur Publishing, we believe in overdelivering way beyond our reader's expectations. Is it okay if we overdeliver?

Here's the deal, we're going to give you an extremely condensed PDF summary of the book which you've just read and much more…

What's the catch? We need to trust you… You see, we want to overdeliver and in order for us to do that, we've to trust our reader to keep this bonus a secret to themselves? Why? Because we don't want people to be getting our exclusive PDF summaries even without buying our books itself. Unethical, right?

Ok. Are you ready?

Firstly, remember that your book is code: "**READ27**".

Next, visit this link: http://bit.ly/exclusivepdfs

Everything else will be self explanatory after you've visited: http://bit.ly/exclusivepdfs.

We hope you'll enjoy our free bonuses as much as we enjoyed preparing it for you!

# Introduction

Mr. Sinek recounts a conversation that he had with an employee of a steel plant in Switzerland. The man gushed about how much he loves his job and his products, continuing on boasting about the products the company sells. The author then asked him WHY he is happy about his current employment—here, the man is, at first, left stumped despite his convincing pitch about the joys of his job.

The author further conversed with the employee, and he eventually elicits the real reasons WHY the man loves his job: He feels that by encouraging people to use only the minimum amount of steel in manufacturing, he is also helping keep our Earth healthier through lessened pollution and waste production. In this way he feels that he is making the world a cleaner and safer place for future generations, including his children. The author paraphrases the man's initial sales pitch and converts it into a statement of WHY: WHY he loves his job and what he does. The man's eyes light up and learns that the best sales pitch is to preface it with the *PURPOSE* of him selling the products and *WHY* the product exists in the first place.

The author explains that it is not WHAT we do or sell that keeps us inspired and gives us passion to do something. What is ultimately important is that we connect what we do to a PURPOSE that resonates deeply with us as individuals. If we are passionate about what we do, the author guarantees that the source of this passion is a deep-seated cause, belief, or purpose. Like the employee, we may not know what it is in words, but we still have it. However, the ability to express ourselves does become important at some point because it makes our vision and purpose even more powerful. Being able to properly article your WHY is also essential.

A common response when people are asked WHY they like what they are doing is **money**. But according to the authors, money is nothing more than a surface WHY. Digging deeper, we must find out WHY we need to make money in the first place. We may think that money is the WHY, but there is a greater motivation behind it. For example, to some, money means more independence. To others it many mean a secure life and being able to provide a good education to their kids. The "WHY" differs from people to people.

The authors also make an important distinction between fulfillment and happiness. They point out that many things can make us happy. In our jobs or business many things can bring us happiness, things such as: completing a project, winning over a new client, getting a promotion – there is an endless list reasons. But feelings of happiness are also temporary emotions.

Do we walk around with the same elation from meeting a sales goal a year ago? Do we still feel the desire to go to a bar and pay for a round of drinks because of a promotion a couple of years back? The answer is NO. This is because the intensity from getting a happy feeling dissipates and even passes with time. But fulfillment lasts because it is deeper, and connects with our personal life goals.

The difference between fulfillment and happiness is the difference between LOVING something and LIKING something.

Also: Fulfillment comes from WHY we do something, while happiness "only" comes from WHAT we do.

For example, we don't necessarily like our children all the time. Think of all the times that we felt exasperated or angry at them. But what we know is that we love our children ALL the time. In the same way, we are not necessarily happy in our jobs every single day, but we can find fulfillment in it if we know that we are making positive changes—whether it be personal or on a larger scale. We can be happy in closing a deal for example, but we will be fulfilled if we know that we are part of a bigger objective with much larger and consequential implications.

3

If we really want to experience passion in what we do and feel that we are part of something much bigger, we need to figure out our WHY—our purpose. The rest of the introduction gives a summary of what to expect in the upcoming chapters and talks about how the Appendices are an important part of getting the most out of the book. The authors advise the reader to treat the book as a "how to" manual and that every chapter consists of steps and a plan of action.

They stress that there is no such thing as a "correct" time frame by which to complete the journey of finding the WHY. The important thing to remember is to stick with each step or section until you are sure that you can move on to the next one. The chapters are meant to be read chronologically and skipping chapters may not be advisable.

The book assumes that you have not read, or do not have prior knowledge of, author Simon Sinek's first book, *Start You Why,* so the authors do provide you with a primer – this should help you better understand all of the different concepts that will be discussed throughout the book.

Shall we delve further into it?

# Chapter 1 - Start with Why: A Primer

Chapter 1 is essentially a summary of Mr. Sinek's first book *Start With WHY*, and it visits the crucial concepts of the Golden Circle and the "Tribe".

The author makes use of the concept of "Golden Circle" to start explaining WHY pioneers and leaders like the Wright Brothers, Martin Luther King, Jr. and Steve Jobs were able to reach heights that other more hardworking, smarter, and well-funded individuals could not.

Essentially, every person's career and organization operates on three levels which is shown as follows:

The diagram shows that on the outer surface, we all know what we do: We know our job specifics, what services we offer or what products we sell. They know their job and they also know HOW to do it well; for example getting product differentiation and helping your service or product stand out from the crowd. However very few people can clearly describe WHY they do what they do.

The reason that makes it is hard to articulate our WHY is that what inspires and motivates goes deeper than the things we usually focus on. WHY *is the belief, cause and purpose.* This is the driving force in every person's career and every organization. It answers the questions of WHY you get up in the morning to go to work and WHY your business or organization exists. If we are not able to articulate the WHY, we will find it harder to motivate not only ourselves, but our customers as well.

Some good salesmen can easily explain WHAT they sell or what they do, after which they explain the underlying HOW. The customer may nod their assent or approval, but if they find a better deal, they will disappear. If there is no palpable difference between Widget 1 and Widget 2, it is hard to sway anyone into choosing the product the salesman represents. Or if the salesman is lucky, they can make the first sale, but the customer may not be inspired to return. There is no loyalty.

This is because loyalty is not based on the benefits or features of the product. Long-lasting relationships and loyalty are based on something more profound. If you can convince a customer that their values and beliefs align with yours then it is very likely that they will want to do business with you not just once, but continuously and steadily. They may even continue their loyalty even if someone sells the same product for a lower price! If you can show customers that you have shared beliefs, then you will have a customer for life.

As an example, this is why Apple is able to maintain a loyal customer base of people who will keep on buying their products over and over even if they are some of the most expensive gadgets available. This is also why fans of some professional sports teams keep on buying season tickets and wear the team jerseys even if they miss the playoffs for many consecutive years.

For this, it helps that we are not 100% percent rational beings, and that a part of us respond more to emotions and feeling. If we were entirely rational rather than being emotional, we would never even think of taking risks that might benefit us in the end. Customers will align themselves emotionally because this "irrational" support comes from a decision-making process that is based on biology more than anything else! The Golden Circle aligns perfectly with the functions of our brain:

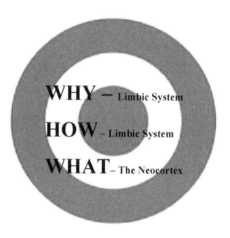

The WHAT of the Golden circle lines up with the neocortex or the outer section of the brain. This area is responsible for our analytical and rational thinking, and enables us to process facts and figures. More importantly, it is responsible for our language ability.

On the other hand, the HOW and the WHY aligns with the brain's middle section: the limbic system. This system is where our feelings come from, along with our decision-making and behavioral processes. It also dictates our tendencies towards loyalty and trust. However, the limbic system, quite unlike the neocortex, does not have the capacity for language. This is why it can be difficult for us to express our WHY; primarily because the brain functions related to it exists in the WHAT and HOW systems. This is why we also sometimes have a hard time expressing our feelings and say things like: "I don't know . . . it just felt right". The same goes for trying to justify why we came to make a business decision.

This is the gap that the authors will help you bridge.

Think of WHY as a versatile tool micro and macro uses. It can be used to see if potential hires are a proper "fit" or whether a new product line is in tune with the company's culture. A WHY also exists for individuals, teams, and entire organizations, and by putting WHY into words makes a culture more tangible, and immediately clarifies which decisions are correct, especially where "gut-feeling" and "hunches" come into play.

There are some parts of a business, such as revenues and profit, which are tangible and easy to measure. But there (sometimes more important) areas that are difficult to measure and are intangible: Hiring that employee who fits, trust, inspiration, vision, etc.

There are many tools to measure for tracking cash flow and keep track of inventory, but tools to measure employee discretionary efforts, culture and vision are not that obvious and apparent. The WHY is that tool. It will bring focus and make the intangible a bit more tangible. It will also allow you to develop a vision to inspire yourself, your colleagues, and your customers. It will show you how WHY can guide you to act on purpose and with purpose.

# Chapter 2 - Discovering Your WHY: An Overview

For most of us, the routine of balancing our daily work and personal life is a lot to deal with. This is why many would rather NOT stop and ask WHY they do what they do. However, it is a necessary step because this WHY brings passion into what we do in life and in work. WHY is not a formula for success but a tool for fulfilling, long-term success. These will come in different ways depending on what you do:

As an entrepreneur, your WHY will allow you to communicate what is unique and singular about your organization to both your customers and employees. Apple, for example, is able to convey that their product more innovative compared to others. Knowing your WHY also facilitates hiring people who "fit" in your organization. A company that has a laser focus on its WHY will want to recruit the right people, whose beliefs mesh well with their own, into its ranks.

If you're an employee, knowing your personal WHY can help you connect with your company, as well as will renew and refresh your passion. If you leave that company finding the next job will be easier because you will most likely land in a company where you will "fit," feel fulfilled, and therefore succeed.

A division or team within a company will most likely have its own subculture. Sometimes the team's contribution to the organization can be powerful, and the people in the team can be connected in a more meaningful and deeper manner to the WHY of the entire organization.

The WHY of a company stems directly from the people who founded it. It is also influenced by their history. However, there are cases wherein the company's purpose changes throughout the course of existence, and would need to be re-discovered once more.

The process of discovery is further discussed in the following three chapters. It tackles all of the steps the organization needs to take, as well as the roles that the people in it will play. The authors break the process down like so:

**Step 1: Gather Stories and Share** – Every person has a concept of who they are and when they are at their best. Getting to the WHY is an origin story. A person should be able to know his or her WHY by talking about the highs and lows in our past, the people that we have influenced, and from these patterns will surface. For individuals, the WHY is formed fully in the late teen years. Our memories must be probed for our defining moments to find the connections.

For teams or groups (Tribes), people who have around for a long time, and especially from the beginning, they WHY will come from the company's founding; from people who will share what make them proud to be a member of the organization. The more stories the better, and the more specific these stories are will allow the team to unearth the tiniest nuggets of insight which will build up hopefully into the big WHY. Participants are asked to come up with at least ten stories, where at least half will need to be explored in detail.

**Step 2: Identify Themes** – The stories that you dig up for yourself and as part of the totality of the stories of your team will eventually yield a pattern or a theme. These can come in the form of insights that you have been "sensing" but have never been expressed or talked about. You will hear yourself say, "That is who I am," or your team will say, "That is our team!" These emerging themes will form the basis of your WHY statement.

13

## Step 3: Draft and Refine a WHY Statement

The WHY statement must be:

Actionable

Expressed in affirmative language that resonates with you

Focused on the effect that you will have on others

Simple and clear

The format is simply:

TO _____ SO THAT _____

In the FIRST BLANK you will fill out what CONTRIBUTION you will make, and the SECOND BLANK will be the IMPACT of your contribution. For example,

**TO** finish every project on time **SO THAT** I will be promoted and be able to afford college tuition for my children. To put this statement in a clearer fashion:

But you should not have a WHY statement like that. Your WHY statement will have to go deeper than that. It has to be relevant in your professional and personal life, and must reflect WHY your friends and co-workers love you and what your value is at work. Remember that there is no separate personal WHY and professional WHY: You are you wherever you are.

Your WHY is not what you sell or what you do. It is not the I-phone, or the steel, or the consulting service that you provide your WHY. Rather it is the tasks that you perform and the decisions that you make that align to deliver your perceived contribution or impact. It is finding the so-called Golden Thread, the recurring ideas and themes that will like your WHATS and HOWS to your WHY.

The Discovery process will help you articulate your WHY, and the **TO** _____ **SO THAT** _____ **format** will codify your true calling.

You will need a good partner or facilitator who will be able to push you to come out of your comfort zone and retrieve the embedded experiences and memories of your true WHY. The authors say that it takes between six minutes and six hours to come up with your WHY statement, but they are sure that after the processes laid out in the coming chapters, you will come up with your own true WHY.

# Chapter 3 – Why Discovery for Individuals

This chapter will provide you with a guide for helping individuals discover their WHY. The steps are relatively simple, here's how to begin:

1. Find your Partner

This is a crucial step which dictates how the rest of the process is going to be. Your partner does not need to be a professional psychologist or therapist, a trained human resources or motivational speaker, or even a good friend. What you need is someone who you feel comfortable enough with since you'll be sharing your memories, thoughts and feelings. Choose someone who can be objective who will hear your accounts for the first time.

Your spouse or your best friend is not recommended because they do have pre-conceived notions about you.

2. Be On the Same Page

Your partner must be advised of the following:

That you are in the Discovery process to extract an origin story;

That he or she needs to be a good listener. Being a good listener is being an ACTIVE listener. The partner must make an effort to acknowledge what you say nonverbally and verbally. The partner must make eye contact, and make you feel that he or she is totally focused on what you are saying.

The partner must also dig deep into your stories, and know when they are only being given surface stories. For example, you may say that visiting your grandparents in their farm every summer was the most important event in your life, and that this shaped your love for nature and the environment. This should not be enough, because there may have been other things during those visits that mattered more. Tell them to try their best to extract the details from you through questions or by helping you remember more things. Appendix 2 summarizes the questions and tips in the process.

Your partner must take detailed notes of the query process.

Your partner must also understand that when you start talking about HOW YOU FEEL rather than WHAT YOU REMEMBER, you are both making great progress. When this happens, your partner must probe deeper into the memory of the feeling.

Negative accounts are important and should not be ignored. Your chosen partner must look at these memories as silver linings to the Discovery process.

Ask the right kind of questions and avoid certain lines of questioning. Ask open-ended questions or those that you cannot respond to with a simple yes or no. Do not ask WHY questions because this trigger the limbic part of the brain which does not generate speaking or language. It is better to ask "what".

Let the partner allow you to struggle to come up with an answer. It is good to listen in silence

3. Find a Time and a Place

This process needs to be done in a quiet place, with minimum of distractions and noise. Doing this at a Starbucks will not provide both of you with a good environment for reflective thought and meaningful interaction. An office during the weekends or a conference room is ideal.

The right time is also crucial. You don't want anyone clock watching for a dinner date or a child's soccer game to keep you on guard as to time. Allot at least 6 hours for this exercise and turn off all means of communications from the outside world if possible.

4. Gather Your Stories

One of the objectives in of this discovery process is to come up with at least five stories that have impacted your life. The more you can come up, with the better. These stories will help you identify the themes and patterns that will help lead to identifying your WHY. There are no such thing as wrong or mundane stories, so you need to think through the many you have in your life with abandon and without hesitation.

Each of your stories should be about a specific moment, place, or time. Think of specific experiences and people in your life that have really shaped who you are today. You may choose an event that was obviously important, such as the day you came up with the idea for your company, or an event that's less obvious, like a defining moment you had with your old boss. The memories may come from school or home, or from your childhood and teen years.

The authors specify what type of stories are most effective in coming up with the WHY:

Peaks and Valleys – These are the highs and lows in your life. Draw a horizontal line a across a sheet of paper and write down the times in your life where felt the happiest or most fulfilled, write this down above this line. Things like your marriage, graduation, or promotion for example are good examples of peaks. The more you value an event as a peak, the higher above the horizontal line it should be.

On the other hand, you also need to write down the valleys under the horizontal line. These are events that you do not necessarily want to remember, but they also shaped who you are by impacting your life in a profound way. The more you consider the event as a valley, write the event lower below the horizontal line.

The authors also provided a number of helpful prompts that can help jog your memory, such as:

The one person in your life who has molded you into what you are today;

An accomplishment that you're really proud of;

A specific moment when you felt unbelievably good after giving yourself up to help someone;

Something that you did that made you think, "I would have done it for free".

Your worst day at work or school that you wish would never happen again.

5. Share Your Stories

This is considered to be the most difficult part of the Discovery process because it is when everything gets a bit more personal. It is never easy sharing stories that mean a lot to us, after all. The key to this sharing process is being specific. Do not hesitate to detail as much as you can, every little bit counts.

For example, going to a grandmother's house every Christmas while evoking wonderful feelings, needs to be drilled down to specific things that are done during that visit, and relatives that are memorable. Having wonderful experiences travelling for business also needs to be broken up into other memorable events, such as meeting new contacts who many give insight not only on their products or services, but about something in their personal lives that have created a deep impression.

6. Identify Your Themes

At this stage of the process, your partner must now apply objectivity when it comes to detailing what common themes arises in your stories. These themes will be the main ideas can be drawn from each story. Examples are:

Helping others;

Seeing the bigger picture;

Pushing the boundaries;

Striving for perfection or greatness;

Helping children or the environment.

Most people tend to have more than one theme to their stories, whilst some only have one. This number matters little to the entire process, so don't focus too much on reaching a certain amount. Keep everything natural and do not force themes onto your stories if it does not fit into it.

7. Draft Your WHY

Once you've managed to find and put together your main themes, the time has come for you and your partner to draft your WHY. You should now prepare two cards or pieces of paper and fill in this statement:

TO _____ SO THAT _____

Take a maximum of five minutes to independently draft this initial WHY statement. Doing this separately is important because you each may articulate the statement differently. The time limit is set in place to help you avoid overthinking things. After the time is up, compare your statements. From here, you can either combine your statements or agree on one overarching WHY. Afterwards, you will need to refine the statement.

## 8. Refine Your WHY Statement

Refining your WHY statement requires you to consult other people who you value. The primary approach is called the "Friend Exercise," where you take your closest friends ONE AT A TIME, and explain the WHY process to them, as well as why their input is important to your process. The first question you need to ask them is: "WHY are you friends with me?" and after some expected generic responses, you should question them further with: "But what specifically is it about me?"

You might find that your friends will come up with new themes related to you. Some may even match what you've already come up with—this is the best result, but getting new input is just as good. It only means that you need to further honing in on the central themes for yourself.

It will be a good idea to put aside your WHY statement for a few days to give you time to let it "settle" and let you get a clear mind and perspective before you revisit it.

# Chapter 4 - Why Discovery for Groups

## *Part 1: The Tribe Approach*

In this chapter the authors describe the process of WHY Discovery for The Tribe. But first, what is a "tribe"? Basically, a tribe is the place where you feel as if you truly belong. It could be any of the following:

Everyone who works in an organization under a CEO is a member of that tribe;

The people who work in a division of a company is a member of the division director or manager's tribe;

The members of a team are members of that team leader's tribe. If you are the director of a division, the people who work in your division.

If your organization's tribe structure isn't as clear-cut like others, you would need to organize your tribe based on what seems right. Also, do remember that an individual may fit into more than one tribe.

The Nested WHY

This is an important concept which deals with interrelated *WHY*s in one organization. Remember that there could be at least 3 levels of WHY in a company:

The WHY of the entire organization, based on the WHY of the founder;

The WHY of divisions or teams within the organization and;

The individual WHY of each associate in the company.

Now think of the organization as a tree. Its foundation and origins are its trunk and its roots. The branches on this tree are the departments and divisions of the organization. Sitting on these branches are nests, which are the teams or subcultures in the tree. Within each nest are the family or individuals.

It is important for an organization to articulate a nested WHY because it gives groups and teams a chance to better understand their contributions as a distinct group towards the overall vision of the company.

The WHY helps guide individuals towards the right nest. This means that we need to look for opportunities in a company that is in line with our WHY. Alternatively, an organization also needs to to identify and articulate its WHY so that it can recruit the right "birds" and give them the proper "nest". This creates an organization that comprised of strong relationships, cultural norms, and common values.

Can a company change its WHY with a leadership change or if the company is bought out by another company?

This cannot happen unless the new leader leads a company whose original purpose has been completely ruined because it has been abandoned, abused, or misused. A new leader just cannot come in and change the WHY and the related themes. The goal of division head or manager is like the organization, and that is to bring the right people into their teams.

For this reason, finding an organization's WHY is even more important because it allows all the parties involved to align their interests towards the fulfillment of their goals. **FACT:** Companies that make a serious effort towards articulating their WHY are also known to be the most innovative and productive, boasting of the highest employment retention rates, and have the highest morale.

Divisions or teams within the organization that try to communicate and commit to their WHY are micro versions of the larger, similarly committed organizations – their morale is high, and their productivity is through the roof.

Apple has been defined as company whose WHY was to challenge the status quo. That WHY was articulated by Steve Jobs, who also proved it when Apple's fortunes changed when he left it (it floundered). His return heralded Apple's resurgence, producing new products such as the iPad, new versions of the I-phone—the very things that made them a household name in the first place.

Its employees are part of this overall culture that's dedicated to innovation and challenging the "norms". Apple hires people with the same ideals and confidence in the job that they do.

The results aren't questionable in any way. We all know that despite the hefty price tag on each one, iPhones remain the top selling mobile devices and has yet to be topped by another brand. Apple's designs are well-loved, their aesthetic is often emulated—but never truly copied. The people who work for the company all do so with pride. From the highest ranks, down to the employees we meet at Apple's shops, the company's WHY is clear.

The Tribe Discovery Workshop

Before anything else, the organization must understand that trying to discover a WHY is not a marketing or a branding exercise. You are not trying to make your organization's product more attractive and saleable. Your goal here, together with the rest of the organization, is to fill in these blanks:

TO _____ SO THAT _____

An organization or a team needs to follow a precise WHY Discovery process which is quite similar to the one meant for individuals. These are as follows:

1. Find Your Facilitator

The only requirement here is TRUST. The facilitator need not be a professional nor do they need to have experience in doing this. Similar to choosing a partner in the individual discovery process, the facilitator only needs to be able to ask probing questions and must possess a natural curiosity.

You can hire the services of someone who has done this before, but even another employee can do it as well. The important thing here is that they have an understanding of the activity's main objective: A WHY needs to be discovered. As much objectivity needs to be applied to the process so an insider in the facilitator role must understand their role.

2. Invite Participants

You need to have the right QUANTITY and QUALITY of participants. If you invite too few, you may not get enough stories to generate a meaningful WHY. If you invite too many, however, you may encounter communication issues within the group and consensus may be difficult to reach. For larger numbers, you will probably need an outside professional to facilitate the Discovery process.

As to the type of participants you should ask to participate, the authors strongly encourage the participation of what they call, "zealots" or those with a passion for the organization. They will come up with deeper reasons for being in the company because their involvement also comes from a deeper emotional level.

You also need to have a balanced representation from all disciplines within the company. Too many accountants or engineers may color the WHY to represent a specific point of view. It is also necessary to include employees from all ranks. While senior or tenured people are important, the voices of newer maybe more passionate people are important. A respected, and preferably senior member of the organization should set the context— this was further discussed in Chapter 5.

3. Choose the Right Place

There should be enough room where the participants can divide themselves into small groups and their discussions interrupt other teams.

The place should also come with the facilities you'll need, such as: a projector, flip charts and whiteboards or blackboards to help the process along. Do provide accessible refreshments for everyone and keep it within the area so they do not have to leave the room (a potential instance for distractions) during the activity.

4. Schedule Enough UNINTERRUPTED Time

For a group of twenty to thirty people, give them four hours or less when it comes to the time limit. Make sure there are no distractions inside the room and that any cell phones and office phones are turned off during the discussion process. Doing this would allow the participants to delve deeper into their thoughts, without anything influencing the way they are thinking.

# Chapter 5 - Why Discovery for Groups

## *Part 2: Talking to the Tribe*

The following steps should be followed for the Tribe Discovery Process:

1. Set the Context (45 minutes to one hour)

The initial speaker will touch on the following:

Explain the reason for the activity;

Explain the concept of WHY and stress the importance of the session and encourage the participants to fully participate;

Have the initial speaker share his or her own WHY story. If the speaker cannot come up with a WHY story, they can take the stories of Apple, the story of Steve, the steel company employee in the Introduction, or the La Marzocco coffee company in Chapter 4.

Divide the participants into pairs, and ask each participant to give a one-minute response to the following question:

What inspired you most when you joined the organization and what inspires you to continue working for the organization?

Ask the pairs to share their thoughts with each other for five minutes, after which each participant will talk for another three minutes. This exercise will help generate conversation and openness.

e. Explain the principle of the Golden Circle on the flip chart or show the TED talk of Simon Sinek explaining it. This can be seen at (http://bit.ly/GoldenCircleTalk).

f. Divide the participants into three groups for the actual running of the Discovery Process.


2. Run the WHY Discovery Process (Two hours to 2-1/2 hours)

The 3 conversations:

These are the three major discussions to determine the themes of the group WHY.

## THE FIRST CONVERSATION - THE HUMAN DIFFERENCE

Duration: 20 minutes, the reporting will be another 30 minutes

Ask the question:

What stories can you tell us about when you were most proud be involved in this organization?

Each team will discuss among themselves answers to the above,

Reporting: Each team will report and discuss on the top three stories that the feel was related in their group. They will post these stories on a flipchart in bullet form.

## THE SECOND CONVERSATION - WHAT'S YOUR CONTRIBUTION?

Duration: 20 minutes, the reporting will be another 15 minutes

Ask the question:
In the stories that you told, can you relate a specific contribution that was made to the lives of others by your organization?

Encourage the teams to use actions verbs like:

To bring together

To build

To connect

To engage

To enjoy life

To enrich

To inspire

To love

To trust

These are examples of your themes. The facilitator should be able to further assist in the process and uncover other themes.

Reporting out: Each team will report their action verbs and the facilitator will write down the actions verbs on a flipchart. Each time an action verb has been mentioned will be marked by an asterisk.

Give everyone 15-minute break

## THE 3RD CONVERSATION - WHAT'S YOUR IMPACT?

Duration: 20 minutes, the reporting will be another 30 minutes

Ask the question:

What did others go on to do or to be because of what your organization?

Ask the teams how other people's lives were affected in a positive way because of the contributions of the organization. The objective of this to build on the stories in the two previous conversations and focus on how other people have been impacted by the organization.

Examples of impact statements include:

People seeing possibilities where they did not before;

People feeling more fulfilled and valued in life;

Building the community.

The facilitator will put up the impact statements on a second flipchart.

## 3. Draft a WHY Statement (35-40 minutes)

The teams will be merged into two equal groups and each one will need to make a presentation about what they think is the WHY statement for the organization. The drafting session will end after come closing remarks.

## 4. Finalizing the WHY Statement

After the two teams present their WHY statements, a group of about six people will work on the WHY statement draft. Note the word "DRAFT." This means that the output should be about 75-80% completed by the end of the session. Over the coming weeks and months, the WHY statement will be further refined and reviewed before it is finally rolled out. In the meantime, the all-important HOWS should be included in the draft.

# Chapter 6 - State Your HOWs

This chapter will close the loop on your Golden Circle. From Chapter 1, the authors discussed the three different parts: the WHAT, HOW, and WHY. In this Chapter, we will complete the Circle.

Through chapters 3 to 5, we were taught about the process of finding the WHY. This "WHY" is aspirational, and expresses who you want to be as a person and organization. The "WHAT" refers to our output – the service or materials that we provide. The "HOW", however, will indicate the way that we behave – how we deliver our product or service and what we do, when we are performing at our best.

Difference Between Core Values and HOWs

For many of us, we've experienced working for organization that proudly announces its "core values" in strategic places in the work area. We remember buzzwords such as the garden-variety "integrity," "diversity," "hard work," "honesty," and "courtesy".

Many organizations talk about these core values, and would also often mistake them for being the company "HOWs" – believing that it represents how they do business. However, these core values are much closer to the WHY rather than HOW an organization delivers its services. For example, "Courtesy" is a value, but is not HOW a company operates. We can however, "Treat people with respect and kindness".

"Treating people with respect and kindness" is a legitimate HOW, which is what *we do* in order to project our core values and our WHY.

HOWs are also thought of as the key to success, and it represents the essential ingredients for the organization to stay at the top of their game. These are the company's strengths, and applies whether you are an organization, a tribe, or an individual.

Decision making

HOWs should be the filters through which important decisions are made. You need to make a list of your HOWs and use this as your standard guide when it comes to addressing certain situations. Just because you know your WHY, it does not mean that things always go smoothly.

Not every project or relationship will perfectly align with your HOWs, but knowing these things would make you more aware of possible tensions before they even arise thus allowing you to curb them long before they become problematic. In this manner, you're also able to predict and prepare for other issues and challenges that you might face along the way.

Where your organization once had to grope in the dark for approaches to issues, the list of HOWs will allow you to articulate what is not working and provide you with an approach or solution.

The HOW Discovery Process

The basic structure of the HOWs will be derived from the themes that were uncovered during the WHY Discovery process. A facilitator will explain the reason for the session, along with the concept of HOW and also stress the importance of the activity when it comes to in determining the day-to-day behavior and operation of the organization.

Here's how the process should go:

1. Revisit the themes uncovered during the WHY Discovery process.

An organization's HOWs are its guiding principles for everyday behavior, and it helps bring the WHY to life. The facilitator will list the themes on a flipchart and discuss each one. For example, an organization's themes may consist of the following:

Always learn from others

Connection

Feeling of safety

Joy

Optimism

Problem solving

Protected loved ones

There's always a solution

## 2. State your HOWs

Remind the participants again that HOWs are not traits or attributes because they are the things that the organization does to actualize the WHY. A HOW must be a guiding principle of HOW to do things, and cannot be very specific, like "The office kitchen needs to be cleaned every afternoon."

Instead, the HOWs should be general guides to action such as the following:

Break new ground

Do what is right

Embrace change

Find the positive in everything

Find the silver lining in every cloud

Learn with a humble mind

Look forward, not backward

3. Provide Context

After you have listed down the HOWs, you need to solidify these by providing a short description of each one and how they might affect the entire organization when applied. The descriptions should not contain a lot of detail and should be as simple as possible. This will make it much easier to deploy in real world situations.

When these HOWs are simply explained and distributed, the organization has completed its Golden Circle.

# Chapter 7 - Take a Stand

## *Do the Things You Say You Believe In*

Now that you have worked so hard to extract your WHY, the next part is actually even harder, and that is to put the WHY in practice. The following steps should be followed:

### 1. Share Your WHY

Just like riding a bicycle, the first few times will be difficult and characterized by wobbliness brought about by fear, uncertainty, and a lack of confidence. In time, however, you'll get better at doing this—and that is an important part of the overall progress. After all, your WHY should be shared with both strangers and those of your tribe who were not participants in the Discovery process.

### Try Sharing With Strangers

For most people, this would be a rather difficult thing to do—especially if they are not the type to open up easily to people they have just met. As such, think of this stage as the metaphorical bicycle. This where you can practice and more acquainted with announcing and describing your personal WHY in a non-structured and informal way.

When people ask you what you do, you can give them your WHY statement in the manner that is comfortable for you at the given moment. By being able to express your WHY in different ways under different conditions, you get more familiar and comfortable with it.

Share with Your Tribe.

In time, people will develop a better connection with their tribe and sharing becomes a much easier task to accomplish. In this case, however, things are a bit more formal. For example, you will need to work on a presentation that will take about 3 to 4 hours. It should also be attended by those who were not involved in the WHY Discovery process. Ask around for people who want to volunteer for the activity. It is a good idea to invite volunteers to attend, this would guarantee that those present during your talk are the ones who are most interested in and passionate about the WHY of the organization.

One of the authors came up with a theory called the "Law of Diffusion of Innovation," which means that those who are enthusiastic about the organization's WHY are also the best people to spread the word to others. If these "innovators" attend, they will most likely spread the WHY statement on their own. The process of sharing should include the following:

Share the Experience (60-75 minutes)

Talk about the WHY Discovery process. Without revealing the WHY and HOWs, discuss the purpose of the process, the Golden Circle, and how the themes, the WHY and the HOWs were developed. Try to make things as simple as possible, but without compromising any of the important details that matter to the whole. If you want to, you can draft this and bring a copy with you—something to use as reference so you don't lose your way as you explain different concepts.

Help Others Own the WHY (45-60 minutes)

Give each participant a card with the WHY statement format in blank and tell them to come up with their own WHY statement as it relates to their contributions to the organization:

TO _____ SO THAT _____

After they have given their own statement, disclose the organization's own statement and explain to the group why they came up with the WHY statement. Make sure that you listen and make notes about every story you're given. You will learn plenty in doing this.

Step 3: Explore New Opportunities (45 minutes)

In this step, the participants would need to discuss how the organization can move forward. This is the time where everyone will be sharing new ideas about products, product delivery, customer service, and other areas where they can fully implement the WHY and the accompanying HOWs. All of which should align with the WHY and the HOW—a challenge that everyone should be able to accomplish with more ease given that they are now better aware of the organization's WHY.

## 2. Live the WHY

Now that you're more away of your WHY and the HOWs, this is a good point for you to begin making important changes to your organization's external and internal communications, products, systems, procedures, policies, and strategies to make sure they align with your WHY. Through it, you should also be able to identify team members that need some help in keeping their individual agenda in tune with that of the company's.

The initial list of things to do will probably be long, but that's normal. Do not let an overwhelming list intimidate you and always remember that any changes you need to do NEED NOT happen immediately. In fact, it would be best to take your time and allow for the different concepts you have discovered to fully sink in.

In doing so, you should be able to come up with better ideas—not just ones derived from impulse. This is especially true for bigger companies where every small decision does create a ripple effect and eventually affects everyone in it. In the meantime, list down your ideas and keep them close.

## 3. Keep the WHY Alive

If we fail to nurture an important idea, it can easily be forgotten, fade, or fizzle. To keep the WHY alive, we must purposely communicate it, commit to living it, and keep it front and center in all of the organization's daily activities.

The danger in any organization is that the WHAT can take over if the WHY is not kept in mind and in the heart. If Apple just sold iPhones for the sake of revenue only, it will become soon apparent to its people and its customers that the main objective is money and not the original focus on being the outsider in the industry.

In turn, they lose the very essence of their company and this can lead to some serious consequences. Instead, make sure that you practice the WHY regularly and do your best to remind everyone of it. In an office where everyone is hyperfocused on their own individual tasks, it can be very easy to lose and forget the WHY.

# Appendix 1 - Frequently Asked Questions

Appendix 1 is useful section which answers the questions that most participants in the Find You WHY live seminars and workshops ask. It provides a great insight into our own doubts and questions about finding the WHY and communicating to the people that matter. The authors clarify certain important points about the WHY:

The WHY is not your family.

You cannot have more than one WHY.

Your WHY doesn't change over time.

You have a WHY whether you want to have one or not.

The WHY is used only for good.

Your WHY is always used in service for others.

You do not have to have a unique WHY or make your WHY different from everyone else's.

Even if you feel that your WHY does not align with your current job, don't quit.

You do not need to compel other people to find their own WHY.

Don't worry if you feel that you do not have the tools or resources you need to have the WHAT and HOW to live your WHY.

For organizations, the following were clarified:

Bigger, more prestigious, and more "interesting" industries will not necessarily have "better" WHY than other organizations. While it may seem that Apple has more interesting stories to share, your facilitator can help your people come up interesting stories that can prove to be passion drivers within your company.

You may have products and services that do not align with your WHY, so take this as an opportunity to renew them or remove them from your inventory altogether. Think of it as spring cleaning.

Never make your company WHY all about making more money.

A company cannot have WHY are different from their sub-units. There are ways to have different departments and divisions to have their WHY align with the major company-wide WHY.

Do not adjust your company's WHY just to fit in with your competitors.

# Appendix 2 - Partner Tips for Individual Why Discovery

This chapter gives tips on how to serve as a partner in a co-worker or friend's personal discovery process. Your role is NOT any of the following: Problem solver, advice giver, mentor, or therapist. Your main role is to be an active listener and cheerleader in the proceedings. The following tips are given:

Focus on feelings;

Ask open-ended questions;

Focus on the person's impact and contribution in each of their stories;

Sit in silence when you listen;

When probing, avoid questions that start with "why";

Wait it out when a person struggles with an answer, don't prod for answers;

Look for silver linings when a person relates an unpleasant or uncomfortable story; and

Ask questions to dig deeper and uncover feelings.

# Appendix 3 - Facilitator Tips for Tribe Why

# Discovery

As we've mentioned earlier, organizations do have the option of hiring a professional facilitator for this activity. However, if you opted to keep things personal by asking a senior officer to do it then there are a few things that they must be aware of. These are not strict rules, of course, and are simply guidelines which should help make everything more convenient, and comfortable for everyone participating.

1. Make sure you have the right setting. Have enough room, light, ventilation, away from all manner of distractions and noise.

2, Make sure you have enough time.

3. Focus participants on how their tribe does business, rather than on what business they do. Keep them away from the WHAT and steer them towards the WHY and HOW.

4. Steer participants away from progress-killing semantic debates. Focus on getting them to surrender ideas without getting stuck on terminology.

5. Avoid questions that start with "why."

6. If a team member shows emotion as they report out their story, dig deeper.

7. Take a firm hand with "story hogs."

8. Keep everything that you hear CONFIDENTIAL.

Confidentiality is important here as not everyone would be keen on getting their personal thoughts exposed. Opening up takes a lot for some people so make sure your facilitator understands this. Sensitivity does play a role in this as well.

A naturally curious person will not force answers out of other people. Instead, they would be able to get the information they require through conversation. Try and discuss this with your chosen facilitator beforehand so you're certain that you're both on the same page when it comes to how to deal with the participants.

# Conclusion

For people who may not have had the pleasure of reading through *Start With Why*, working through *Find Your Why* can still be a very rewarding and profitable exercise. The authors have made sure that the spirit of the first book was kept in *Find Your Why*, as is the spirit of Simon Sinek's TED Talk on the subject almost ten years ago. While they make many references to the first book, a person encountering the WHY for the first time will not lose any of the original points made.

Note that I used the words, "working through *Find Your Why*, as opposed to "reading *Find Your Why*". More 50% of the book was designed to provide a detailed and step-by-step guidance on the WHY Discovery (and for that matter, the HOWs discovery) with a bunch of great examples thrown in.

Workbook format or not, the significance of knowing your WHY cannot be overstated. An organization that is serious about meeting its objectives whether humanitarian or monetary, must understand that knowing its WHY is invaluable and indispensable. It is the best way to find the right people to recruit, and greatly improves their retention potential. It is also a way to appear consistent and authentic to both insiders and outsiders.

If you are responsible for developing strategy, engagement, or like programs for your organization, this is a must read. As an individual, you owe it to yourself to know your inner WHY and find out what kind of organization you might fit and where you would fit in an organization.

While the book may not be classified as "motivational" because of its format, there is enough in it to convince anyone that finding your WHY will greatly improve your life and more importantly, the life of others. That should be more than enough reason to get yourself motivated!

# FREE BONUSES

**<u>P.S. Is it okay if we overdeliver?</u>**

Here at Readtrepreneur Publishing, we believe in overdelivering way beyond our reader's expectations. Is it okay if we overdeliver?

Here's the deal, we're going to give you an extremely condensed PDF summary of the book which you've just read and much more...

What's the catch? We need to trust you... You see, we want to overdeliver and in order for us to do that, we've to trust our reader to keep this bonus a secret to themselves? Why? Because we don't want people to be getting our exclusive PDF summaries even without buying our books itself. Unethical, right?

Ok. Are you ready?

Firstly, remember that your book is code: "**READ27**".

Next, visit this link: http://bit.ly/exclusivepdfs

Everything else will be self explanatory after you've visited: http://bit.ly/exclusivepdfs.

We hope you'll enjoy our free bonuses as much as we enjoyed preparing it for you!

CPSIA information can be obtained
at www.ICGtesting.com
Printed in the USA
LVHW041349170619
621462LV00001B/64

9 781646 151264